The Adventures of Pierre the French Bulldog: A Tail of Excitement

This is a work of fiction. Names, characters, businesses,
organizations, places, events, and incidents either are the
product of the author's imagination or are used fictitiously. Any
resemblance to actual persons, living or dead, events, or locales is
entirely coincidental.

The following trademarked terms are mentioned in this book:
Mohamed El Afia. The use of these trademarks does not
indicate an endorsement of this work by the trademark owners.
The trademarks are used in a purely descriptive sense and all
trademark rights remain with the trademark owner.

Cover design by el Emma afia.

This book was typeset in Emma afia.

First edition, 2023.

Published by Emma Afia.

Chapter 1: A Curious Bulldog

- Introduction of Pierre the French Bulldog and his owner, Sophie
- Pierre discovers a hole in the fence and wants to explore the forest
- Sophie warns Pierre about the dangers of the forest, but he can't resist

Chapter 2: Meeting the Forest Animals

- Pierre enters the forest and meets a wise old owl
- The owl warns Pierre about the forest's dangers and gives him advice
- Pierre encounters a mischievous raccoon who tries to trick him

Chapter 3: Lost in the Forest

- Pierre gets separated from the raccoon and gets lost in the forest
- He encounters a friendly deer who helps him find his way back
- Pierre learns the importance of listening and being careful in new environments

Chapter 4: Overcoming Obstacles

- Pierre and the deer come across a rushing stream they need to cross
- Pierre uses his cleverness and resourcefulness to create a bridge and cross safely
- They encounter a group of unfriendly birds who try to attack them

Chapter 5: Home at Last

- Pierre and the deer reach the edge of the forest and find Sophie waiting for them
- Sophie is happy to see Pierre and thanks the deer for helping him
- Pierre learns the value of friendship and being loyal to those he cares about.

Chapter 1: A Curious Bulldog

Pierre the French Bulldog was a curious and adventurous dog who loved to explore the world around him. One day, while playing in his backyard, he noticed a small hole in the fence that separated his yard from the dense forest beyond.

Pierre's owner, a kind-hearted girl named Sophie, had warned him about the dangers of the forest and cautioned him not to venture too far. But Pierre was too curious to resist the allure of the mysterious hole.

As soon as Sophie left the yard, Pierre darted through the hole and into the woods, eager to see what secrets it held.

Chapter 2:

Meeting the Forest

Animals

As Pierre made his way through the forest, he encountered a wise old owl perched on a branch high above him. The owl noticed Pierre and called down to him, "Hello there, young pup. What brings you to our forest?"

Pierre explained that he was just exploring and was curious about the world beyond his backyard. The owl warned him of the dangers of the forest and gave him some advice on how to stay safe.

As Pierre continued on his journey, he stumbled upon a mischievous raccoon. The raccoon tried to trick Pierre into following him deeper into the forest, but Pierre was too clever for him and managed to escape his clutches.

Despite the obstacles he encountered, Pierre continued to explore, eager to discover what other creatures and wonders the forest held.

Chapter 3: Lost in the Forest

As Pierre journeyed further into the forest, he began to lose his sense of direction. He realized that he was lost and didn't know how to find his way back to Sophie's house.

Just as Pierre was starting to panic, he heard a rustling in the bushes nearby. Out stepped a friendly deer who noticed Pierre's distress and offered to help him find his way back home.

The deer led Pierre through the forest, showing him how to navigate through the trees and avoid dangerous areas. Along the way, Pierre learned an important lesson about the importance of being careful and listening to those who are more experienced. As they walked, Pierre and the deer chatted and got to know each other better. Pierre felt grateful to have made a new friend and was hopeful that they would soon find their way back to Sophie's house.

Chapter 4: Overcoming Obstacles

Pierre and the deer soon came upon a rushing stream that blocked their path. The stream was too deep and too fast for Pierre to cross, and he began to worry that they would never make it back home.

But Pierre's cleverness and resourcefulness soon kicked in. He used nearby rocks and sticks to build a makeshift bridge, allowing him and the deer to safely cross the stream.

As they continued their journey, Pierre and the deer encountered a group of unfriendly birds who began to swoop down and attack them. Pierre quickly realized that they were protecting their territory, and he came up with a plan to distract the birds while he and the deer made their escape.

With Pierre's quick thinking and bravery, they were able to overcome these obstacles and continue on their journey back to Sophie's house.

Chapter 5: Home at Last

Finally, after a long and eventful journey, Pierre and the deer reached the edge of the forest and saw Sophie waiting for them. She had been worried sick about Pierre and was relieved to see him safe and sound.

Pierre bounded towards Sophie, tail wagging with joy. Sophie scooped him up in her arms and hugged him tightly, grateful to have her furry friend back home.

The deer stayed nearby, watching the heartwarming reunion between Pierre and Sophie. Sophie thanked the deer for helping Pierre find his way back home, and the two of them exchanged a grateful nod of understanding.

As Pierre settled back into his familiar surroundings, he realized that while he loved to explore and discover new things, there was no place like home. He felt happy and content to be back with Sophie and grateful for the adventures he had experienced.

And with that, Pierre curled up in Sophie's lap, content in the knowledge that he was loved, safe, and happy.

The End

This is a work of fiction. Names, characters, businesses, organizations, places, events, and incidents either are the product of the author's imagination or are used fictitiously. Any resemblance to actual persons, living or dead, events, or locales is entirely coincidental.

The following trademarked terms are mentioned in this book: Mohamed El Afia. The use of these trademarks does not indicate an endorsement of this work by the trademark owners. The trademarks are used in a purely descriptive sense and all trademark rights remain with the trademark owner.

Cover design by el Emma afia.

This book was typeset in Emma afia.

First edition, 2023.

Published by Emma Afia.

Made in the USA
Monee, IL
20 November 2023

46981170R00017